The Need for Change

Change

Four Trends Endangering

Every Organisation

...and what to do about them

Stuart Corrigan

Published in this paperback edition in 2012 by:
Triarchy Press
Station Offices
Axminster
Devon. EX13 5PF
United Kingdom

+44 (0)1297 631456
info@triarchypress.com
www.triarchypress.com

A catalogue record for this book is available from the British Library.

ISBN: 978-1-908009-74-6

Contents

FOREWORD v

INTRODUCTION: THE NEED FOR CHANGE IN A
TOUGH ECONOMY 1

CURRENT BUSINESS TRENDS 3

Trend 1: The Rise of the Complaint Culture 3

Trend 2: Reputation Exposure 10

Trend 3: Declining Staff Morale 17

Trend 4: Instant Gratification – The Need for Speed 22

WHAT TO CHANGE – 4 KEY STRATEGIES 27

Strategy 1: Be obsessed with customer happiness 27

Strategy 2: Be obsessed with staff happiness 32

Strategy 3: Be obsessed with speed of response 37

Strategy 4: Be obsessed with constant innovation 43

HOW TO CAUSE THE CHANGE 47

CATEGORISING SERVICES FOR FASTER DIAGNOSIS ... 63

APPLYING THE MODEL 65

Case Study 1: A Project System 65

Case Study 2: A 'Put-in-to-process' System 71

Case Study 3: A Single-touch System 76

SUMMARY 78

For Mum, Dad and Aunt Net

Foreword

A little book with a big message

Here Stuart Corrigan reminds management of things we feel we know, and does so with compelling evidence. More importantly he points us away from common and superficial remedies; instead introducing a single powerful remedy that, while counterintuitive is, nevertheless, both proven and profound.

A wake-up call for those who want to survive and thrive.

Professor John Seddon

* * * * *

What others have said about this book:

"Stuart Corrigan has done all busy and stressed managers a real favour with this book.

It is short, crisp, full of evidence and spells out the issues that need our focus and action. In addition, he also generously and openly tells us how to make his approach work in our own workplace.

This book offers its readers the chance to leave positive transformational legacies."

Jim Mather, Former Scottish Minister for Enterprise

* * * * *

"...very well written. It's easy on the eye, fun and interesting to read. ...I've stepped away from it remembering what the messages are - now, there are not many books which can do that."

Eileen Flockhart, Business Change Manager,
Lothian and Borders Police

Introduction: The need for change in a tough economy

As I write, recession continues to take its toll on the economies of the UK and other European countries – as well as much further afield. Accountants Grant Thornton report that confidence in the UK's retail and wholesale, manufacturing and engineering and property sectors is at an all-time low.

Life is no better for the public sector. By 2015, UK government agencies are required to save £81 billion and 480,000 jobs.

In short everyone has to somehow tighten their belts.

The larger economy is not something that individual managers have much control over. But there are some places where you can make a real difference. In the next few chapters I'm going to highlight four trends that you need to take into consideration whether you are in the public or the private sector.

So this book is designed to help service organisations big and small, public and private, improve their service, reduce their costs, improve the morale of their staff and, for those that need it, become more competitive.

In his recent book *Outliers*, Malcolm Gladwell, the *New York Times* journalist, identified one major factor in whether an individual becomes successful or not: the ability to challenge conventional assumptions.

The advice offered here on how to address these four trends will challenge some of the conventional assumptions most of us harbour about to how to design and manage the way we deliver customer service. I hope you are able to open your mind to it because ultimately survival in business, like everywhere else, is about being practical, not hidebound.

S. Corrigan

Stuart Corrigan

Current Business Trends

Trend 1: The Rise of the Complaint Culture

On the 23rd of April 1985 the Coca Cola Company announced that old Coke was to be replaced with 'New Coke'. Extensive testing showed that 55% of tasters preferred New Coke. Company Chairman Roberto C. Goizueta explained that New Coke was "smoother, rounder yet bolder" making it sound more like fine wine than fizzy pop.

But the world wasn't happy. At the height of the consumer rebellion, customers were calling to complain at a rate of 1,500 calls per day, 4 times the normal level of calls[1] (at Vanguard, calls like this are known as 'failure demand'). *Time* magazine later voted it number 2, after the Segway, in its list of the '50 Worst Inventions of all time'[2]. Simply put, when Coca Cola announced that it was changing the taste of the world's number one soft drink, it failed to foresee the anger the news would create. And some people took it very personally.

Gay Mullins, a resident of Seattle, Washington, was so incensed that he started the 'Old Cola Drinkers of America League' and set up a hot-line for disgruntled and depressed customers. And it mattered not a jot to Gay Mullins that in 2 blind tests he had said he preferred New Coke to Old Coke. Such was the strength of public opinion and level of complaints that in July of the same year New Coke was

---

1   *Time Magazine* (24/06/1985) 'All AFizz over the new Coke' http://ti.me/TPchange1

2   *Time Magazine* (27/05/2010) 'The 50 Worst Inventions' http://ti.me/TPchange2

yanked from the shelves and 'Classic Coke' put back in its place.

This episode proved to be a watershed for customer service. Since then it's become more and more common for consumers to have a rant. And levels of complaints, especially for poor service, are continuing to grow.

For example in 2010:

- The UK Financial Services Ombudsman received 200,000 complaints about service. 500 complaints forms were downloaded from its website on Christmas Day alone.
- In the public sector, complaints to the Scottish Public Services Ombudsman increased by 12% – the highest level in the office's 7 year history.
- The UK's Telecommunications Industry Ombudsman received over 59,000 complaints – an increase of 14,000 on the year before.
- Even the UK's Nursing and Midwifery Council reported that complaints against nurses and midwives had increased by 57% in the space of a year.

But does it matter? Do any real financial consequences result from delivering what customers perceive as bad service? It would seem that they do and the results don't make comfortable reading.

The global cost of bad service

The first large-scale survey of the impact of bad customer service, carried out in 2009, estimated total annual losses of $338.5 billion[3].

---

3   Genesys Alcatel-Lucent survey, 02/12/2009. To request a complete copy of the findings of "The Cost of Poor Customer Service: The Economic Impact of the Customer Experience and Engagement", email press@genesyslab.com

The survey was conducted by Genesys Labs in collaboration with data analysts at Ovum, and covered 16 industrialised countries, including the UK, the USA, China, Brazil, Germany, Russia, France, Italy, The Netherlands, Australia, India and Canada. Losses were defined as transactions taken to a competitor - accounting for 63% of the total - or ones abandoned entirely, accounting for the remaining 37%.

8,800 consumers were involved in the survey. They were asked how their interactions via the internet, call centres and mobile phones affected their purchasing decisions.

The survey showed that the hardest hit of all industries were financial services, cable and satellite TV providers and telecommunications. Even traditionally 'safe' sectors are now starting to see major losses though 'customer churn'.

However when you look at the actual losses, they tell a staggering story. In the past year, financial services lost over $44 billion in revenue. TV providers suffered losses of more than $36 billion, and telecommunications saw more than $69 billion walk out of the door to competitors.

Of course, you can argue that some of those disgruntled customers are also walking away from other businesses and coming to yours. But the cost of losing an established customer and welcoming a new one is significantly higher than the cost of just retaining a customer.

The local impact of bad service

Our own research has found much the same story. However, not only have we found that there are financial consequences resulting from poor service, but the human aspect of service delivery also needs to be considered.

A simple place to start to study the consequences of poor service is the humble contact centre. In two studies of call centres in both the public sector and private sector we found that better service ultimately costs the organisation less. The reason is that poor service erodes capacity, which then increases costs.

We found, for example, that many calls to call centres fall into the category of what John Seddon calls 'failure demand' (that is, demand caused by a failure to do something or failure to do something right for the customer[4]). Failure calls take longer to deal with than other calls and thus cost more. For example, in one utilities company a failure demand call such as 'Why is my bill wrong?' cost the company an equivalent of £2.24 per call, whereas a value demand call like, 'Can I open a new account with you?' cost only £1.84 per call. We found the same in a local government contact centre where the time spent on a value demand call was only 4 mins 40 seconds compared to a failure demand call which took, on average, 6 mins 30 seconds.

Then there's the human impact of bad service. In a study of the delivery of a grants and adaptations service for the elderly and disabled we found it was not unusual for a customer to wait over 3 years to get an adaptation to their home (level floor shower, stairlift, etc.). Unfortunately, around 8% of customers died whilst waiting for the service. Whilst it would be wrong to conclude there was any direct connection between the wait for the service and the customer death, it would be fair to assume that the customer could have been made much more comfortable in their final years if they had been given better service. Additionally, once customers got their service they were able to stay living in their own home longer, instead of

---

4   J. Seddon (2003) *Freedom from Command and Control*, Buckingham: Vanguard Press

having to go into a funded care home. Faster service also meant that there was less likelihood of a home accident leading to an admission to hospital, at an incalculable human cost but a very calculable cost to the taxpayer of over £400 pounds per night. I'll go into more depth about what we did to help them later in the book.

Q: So why does bad service cost more?
A: Failure demand, stress and reputation

As previously stated, the first reason bad service costs more is that unhappy customers consume more of an organisation's capacity. If they didn't get what they wanted the first time they'll be back. Thus if lots of people are tied up dealing with those repeat contacts (failure demand), it affects their capacity to serve other customers, and eventually more capacity has to be found through costly overtime or increases in staff numbers.

In an early consulting job with a bank we were asked to discover why, despite the claim that their new call centres would save money, costs were rising. The reason was that over 50% of the bank's calls were failure demand, hence additional capacity constantly had to be added, leading to higher costs. But, because managers did not differentiate between value demand and failure demand, the assumption was that more calls would bring in more revenue. More calls did, in fact, mean more money, but not in the way the managers wanted!

Another example comes from a client organisation that provides industry certification and accredited membership. It looked at the customer demand in its call centre and found that only 32% of the calls it was receiving were of the type it wanted/expected.

Approximately 68% of the calls into its contact centre were self-generated by failures in its system. And it was paying for it in terms of rising costs, poor service and high staff absence.

In our experience, in organisations that deliver poor service, between 40% and 85% of customer contact demands are failure demand. In such cases the opportunities for making cost savings are significant.

Another reason for the high cost of poor service is the impact that rework (constantly having to go back and put things right for the customer) has on staff stress and morale. Think about it: if customers are shouting at you all day long it's eventually going to get to you.

But making a change can make a big difference. Take for example one Glenrothes contact centre. It was suffering from high sickness rates, high staff turnover and poor customer service. An analysis of the work design revealed that staff were dealing with high levels of failure demand. Add in the additional factors of imposed targets, average wrap-up times and high abandon rates and it soon became obvious why staff were stressed. In addition they were often unable to deal with customer requests as they did not have the relevant technical expertise.

The work was redesigned on systems thinking principles – knowledge of customer demand was used to determine the expertise required to serve customers. Technical staff were removed from the back office and put in the contact centre to provide expertise at the front line. If a member of staff got a call they could not deal with they would raise their hand and the expert would help them, transferring knowledge to all staff in the process. This reduced the levels of customer re-calls and instantly reduced pressure on staff. Targets were replaced with daily sessions where staff and management focused on what mattered to customers and on solving problems they encountered frequently – to make it easier for staff to give customers what they wanted.

As a result, the ability to deal with customer enquiries at the initial point of contact improved and sickness rates fell to less than half the industry average. Capacity increased by 30%. The organisation went on to improve back office flows and made a further £1 million reduction in operating costs over 3 years.

Then there's the impact of bad service on customer loyalty. A recent survey found that 21% of bank customers switching accounts to other providers cited poor service and unmet expectations[5]. Customer tolerance levels are decreasing and their reactions are getting stronger. Voting with our feet is rapidly becoming the new cultural norm.

And for those who think they can get away with poor service if they lower their prices... more than half of consumers worldwide (54%) say that they are not willing to compromise on levels of customer service, product options, product quality and frequency of communications with companies in exchange for lower prices[6].

Then there's the final impact of poor service: the impact that it has on your reputation. As you'll read in the next chapter, reputation exposure is another important trend that threatens all organisations.

---

5   02/03/2011, http://bit.ly/TPchange3

6   *The 2010 Accenture Global Consumer Research Survey*, http://bit.ly/TPchange4

Trend 2: Reputation Exposure

My eldest son has just passed his driving test so we've been on the lookout for his first car. A friend manages a garage and called to say he had a great deal on a yellow Ford KA. I called my son to let him know – here's the exact transcript of his reply, "Aw c'mon dad it's a nice thought 'n all that but I've got my rep' to think of - seriously a *yellow* Ford KA?" He later explained all the different ways that his friends could dis' him for having said car:

- By text
- On Twitter
- On Facebook
- On MySpace
- On BEBO
- On their blogs
- On YouTube

(By the way, he's got a white Toyota Yaris and his reputation is seemingly intact.) If you're a teenager then your reputation is a big deal, but – let's be honest – it always has been. What's changed for them recently is that there are more and more ways of being publicly slagged off. And it's not just teenagers that are suffering. Businesses big and small are now seeing the very real impact of negative social media on the reputations of their brands.

Reputation management is now a big issue

As early as 2001, researchers from Silberman College of Business found that reputation management was gaining ground as the driving philosophy behind corporate public relations[7]. A tactic previously more applied to the less publically acceptable behaviours of Hollywood starlets is now being applied to complaints against your average service provider.

In the old days the biggest concern was that a disgruntled customer would tell 16 of their friends. In today's internet-driven world, if a customer has a bad experience they can post their comment on any of the big feedback/complaint blogs and, within hours, millions of customers and potential customers may know the not so good, the bad and the ugly about your company.

Many take it a step further. In Scotland, if you search for 'Edinburgh Audi' online you'll see that one disgruntled customer has set up a website solely to share his bad experiences with the car dealer. So far over 12,800 people have visited the site. And he's by no means alone in creating a complaint site. More importantly, it is suggested that if in search results a company website has a negative result directly below it, up to 70% of surfers will click on the negative result first rather than the company website.

But many customers have even bigger plans when it comes to getting their own back.

The revenge of the disgruntled customer

In a famous case of disgruntlement Dave Carrol, a musician, put his guitar in the hold of a United Airlines flight. The £3,000 guitar got broken and, despite 9 months of repeated attempts to complain, Mr Carrol was ignored. Deciding that

---

7   J. Hutton, M. Goodman, J. Alexander, C. Genest (2001) 'Reputation Management, the new face of corporate public relations?', *The Public Relations Review* Volume 27 issue no 3. http://bit.ly/TPchange5

no-one puts Davey in the corner he penned a song about the broken guitar and put in on YouTube.

The video was posted on Monday 6th July, 2009. In its first 23 hours, viewers of "United Breaks Guitars" had posted 461 comments on YouTube, most of them also maligning the airline. The video then quickly went viral, with 24,000 views by Tuesday night. The story made the *LA Times* and then most newspapers and TV stations in the US and the UK. To date the video has been seen by nearly 12 million people[8].

As you can imagine, United were suddenly quick to respond. "This has struck a chord with us, and we've contacted him directly to make it right," said a spokeswoman for United. (She also said she "loved" the video.) But it was too late.

Did it hurt the airline? You bet it did! Within four days of the video being posted, the company's stock price had fallen by 10%, costing shareholders $180 million[9]. Better, it would seem, to have a culture where the baggage handlers didn't throw guitars around in the first place.

But it's not only airlines that need to be concerned. Companies that fail to deal with complaints to the satisfaction of their customers could easily find they have their own 'United Breaks Guitars' PR nightmare. And it's not only the one-time complainant that companies need to worry about, it's the problem that caused the complaint that should concern them because it could recur and recur and recur.

---

8   http://www.youtube.com/watch?v=5YGc4zOqozo

9   C. Ayres (22/07/2009) 'Revenge is a dish best served cold – on YouTube', *Times Online.* http://thetim.es/TPchange6

News of your misdemeanours is now permanent

Even if you diligently fix the problem (which I'd strongly recommend) you can still be in trouble. In the good old days, if 16 people had got a hold of your tale of woe it might have been remembered for a week or two... until another juicy titbit came along. But today your bad rep can haunt you permanently. Dave Carrol's guitar video on YouTube was posted in 2009, yet it still attracts hundreds of visitors every day. At the time of writing, two years later, if you search for United Airlines in Google, Dave's rant still comes up at the top of page 2.

So a new trend has been born. Now that it's understood that a brand isn't just about marketing, it's marketing and reputation combined, many companies see the issue as so serious that they're investing time and money in the proactive management of their online character.

Woburn Safari Park has admitted using an online 'reputation management' company to bury headlines that might damage its business. In June 2010, several newspapers ran stories that the zoo had received a poor inspection report from the Department for Environment, Food and Rural Affairs. The park later disclosed that it had hired the services of online reputation manager Keith Griggs.

Mr Griggs said he started working for "a wildlife park" in July 2010, when three of the first ten results on Google for Woburn were news articles about the allegations. Within a week there were no longer any links to critical stories on the first page of results, according to *The Times*. A few months later we were told there was only one negative report in the first five pages of results (until the papers got hold of the news).

This is just one example of the many organisations that now understand the impact a bad reputation is likely to have on current and prospective clients' interactions with them and on their bottom line, and that are using this new type of PR to boost their positive image and hide negative stories[10].

Others agree that your online brand matters. Herb Tabin, CBS News Tech Correspondent, entrepreneur, and co-author of the book *Do It Yourself Online Reputation Management*, says: "In business and in life you're a brand, so I think that it's important that you're proactive in the sense that you have to have info out there that you want people to see. You want to have a good part in forming your own reputation online."

But just how powerful is social media in spreading information about your reputation?

Social media is unquestionably a powerful influencing factor in how your organisation is viewed. 90% of consumers online trust recommendations from people they know; 70% trust opinions of unknown users[11]. In fact 41% of Europeans claim to have changed their mind about what brand to buy as a result of researching choices online[12].

According to Blogpulse, 77% of UK users use blogs to inform their purchasing decisions. Facebook is now more visited than Google and 30 billion pieces of content are shared on Facebook every month. 25 billion tweets were sent in 2010

---

10   A. Bloxham (01/06/2011) 'Woburn Safari Park uses online reputation managers to bury damaging headlines on Google' *The Telegraph*, http://tgr.ph/TPchange7

11   Nielsen Global Online Consumer Survey (July 2009) http://bit.ly/TPchange8

12   EIAA Mediascope survey. (Mediascope Europe, November 2008) http://slidesha.re/TPchange9

and 84% of internet users view videos online, with 2 billion being watched every day[13].

And internet usage is still growing. In fact it has grown by 14% since 2009 and in 2011 it was estimated there are now over 1.9 billion internet users worldwide. Add 152 million blogs and that's a heck of a lot of people writing and reading – amongst other things – about products and service!

The simple conclusion is that a) there's a boatload of people writing, tweeting and talking about products and services (including yours) online and b) there's another boatload of people trusting the first group's information to guide their purchasing decisions... hence if your service or product is failing, a lot of people are going to know about it fast!

On the other hand if you offer a good service and good customer interactions, it pays off. Brands with the highest positive 'social media activity' (including blogs and reviews) increase their revenues by as much as 18%[14] and 69% of companies using Web 2.0 say they have gained measurable business benefits[15].

The relationship between service and reputation

So how do you go about deliberately building a good reputation? A bit like eating an elephant – one bit at a time. Except that a reputation is built one transaction at a time.

A transaction is any point of contact along the service chain between the customer and the supplier. For example, a

---

13   Data from Omobono digital brand engagement. http://www.omobono.com/

14   *Media Post News*, July 2009

15   *McKinsey Quarterly*, September 2009

point of transaction in the United Airlines debacle was the point where the baggage was transferred from the trolley to the plane. Even though the customer is not present they can take a view of the quality of that transaction based on the condition of their luggage when it appears on the luggage belt. Other points of transaction would include purchasing a ticket, check-in, the boarding procedure, interactions with cabin staff, etc.

At every point of transaction the customer takes a view of the quality of the service. Eventually the accumulation of customers' experiences of those transactions is communicated socially and creates a reputation and the reputation then merges with marketing efforts and becomes the brand image in the mind of the public. What many businesses still haven't figured out, however, is that managing reputation is simply about managing those individual touch points with the business.

So keep an eye out online for what people are saying about you, because it's one thing getting ribbed by your peers because you're a 17-year-old driving a yellow Ford KA, it's another if 12 million people are watching a Country and Western singer lament your crappy service whilst your shareholders bleed $180 million!

Trend 3: Declining Staff Morale

Does it pay to keep staff happy?

The *Daily Record* recently reported that more than 3,000 NHS staff in Scotland are off work on long-term sick leave. Across the UK as a whole the CBI reported that in 2010 an estimated 160 million working days were lost through sickness at a cost of £16.8 billion.

The UK Health and Safety Executive estimates that at least half of sickness days lost are related to work-place stress.

In fact over half of Britain's employees are unhappy at work, with over a third of them seriously considering leaving their jobs, according to research by Mercer that reveals an increasing level of employee disengagement that should be of deep concern to employers. The data is based on Mercer's 2011 'What's Working'™ research amongst 2,400 UK workers in over 1,000 private sector organisations – part of a global survey of nearly 30,000 employees in 17 countries.

The feedback from employees also shows a marked decline in commitment and job satisfaction since 2006, when a similar survey was conducted. Only 61% currently say their work gives them a feeling of personal accomplishment compared to 70% in 2006, whilst commitment to their company has declined from 59% to 52%. Just 55% feel proud to work for their organisation compared to 60% in 2006.

Our own surveys at Vanguard found much the same result. We are interested in the impact of job design on the motivation of front-line staff. In both a financial services company and a local authority we found that the levels of stress and motivation (due to the repetitive nature of the jobs and imposition of targets) were equivalent to working in a factory bottling hall.

In 2010, Prime Minister David Cameron announced plans to measure the nation's happiness, saying that GDP was "an incomplete way of measuring a country's progress", and quoting former US attorney general, Bobby Kennedy, who said that GDP measured everything "except that which makes life worthwhile".

"More than 80% of British workers lack any real commitment to their jobs, and a quarter of those are 'actively disengaged,' or truly disaffected with their workplaces." These are amongst the troubling findings of the Gallup Organisation's Employee Engagement Index survey, which examines employee engagement levels in several countries, including the United Kingdom.

The fact is that the majority of the UK's 27 million employees – who work the longest hours in Western Europe – are uninspired at work. Gallup estimates that actively disengaged workers cost the British economy more than £37 billion per year due to low employee retention, high absentee levels and low productivity.

Gallup calculated the percentages within the total British workforce for three categories of employees: 19% are "engaged" – loyal, productive and find their work satisfying; 61% are "not engaged" – employees who aren't psychologically committed to their roles and may leave if an opportunity presents itself; and 20% are "actively disengaged" – disenchanted with their workplace. Actively disengaged employees are often vocal or militant in showing their negative attitude toward their work and their employer[16].

What's more, only 13% of actively disengaged employees and 32% of unengaged employees would recommend their company's products or services to others, compared to 78% of engaged employees. And although 67% of engaged employees actively advocate their organisation as a place to work, only 19% of their unengaged colleagues and a paltry 3% of actively disengaged workers would recommend their workplace to others.

Levels of engagement in the UK compare unfavourably with those in the United States, where 27% of workers are engaged or fully committed to their jobs - a difference of 8 percentage points. However the percentage of engaged workers in the UK compares favourably with engagement levels in Germany and France (12% each), Japan (9%) and Singapore (6%), all of which are markedly lower than those in the UK.

Heidi Waddington, associate director at Badenoch and Clark said: "Economic uncertainty... has put tremendous pressure on employees. It is important that organisations foster an environment where their employees are able to develop a strong sense of self-worth. Failure to do so may result in loss of talent, which in turn will lead to loss of potential revenue"[17].

But does low morale really matter?

I'm sitting in a local authority staff canteen as I write this piece for the book. I have all the research laid out in front

---

16 P. Flade (11/12/2003) *The Gallup Management Journal*

17 J. Williams (Jan 2011) *HR Magazine*

of me but am searching for a opener. As I stare into a blank wall I catch a conversation between two council employees. Let's call them Jack and Jim.

Jim: *How are you today?*

Jack: *Not so bad but that's me done my bit for today, I started at 6.30am and now it's a quarter past eight (am). Time for a long rest!*

Jim: *Me too, I'm bored so I'm off for a drive, I've invented a reason to get out for a couple of hours...*

A high proportion of my work is done in the public sector and I've met many people who love their work and do a great job. But the fact is that there are many more who are disengaged, which leads to stress and low morale. And low morale carries a high price tag. In the US, where more research has been done, the conclusions are startling. Gallup estimates that the 22 million actively disengaged US employees are costing the American economy as much as $350 billion per year in lost productivity including absenteeism, illness and other problems (like those in the conversation above) that occur when employees are unhappy at work.

Leaders who fail to address morale issues in the workplace face the following: decreased productivity, increased rates of absenteeism and associated costs, increased conflicts in the work environment, increased complaints, dissatisfied consumers and increased employee turnover rates and costs associated with hiring and training replacement staff[18].

A government study in the UK also suggests that the impact of engagement (or disengagement) can manifest itself

---

18   N. Fink, MSL Program, Roberts Wesleyan College, Westside Drive, Rochester, NY 14624

through productivity and organisational performance, outcomes for customers of the organisation, employee retention rates, organisational culture and advocacy of the organisation and its external image[19].

The conclusion to be drawn from this research is indisputable: disengaged and unhappy workers have an adverse effect on profits, customer loyalty, repeat business and operating expense. It truly pays to make sure that your organisation makes workers happy and committed.

19 DTZ Consulting & Research (2007) 'Employee engagement in the public sector: a review of the literature'

Trend 4: Instant Gratification – The Need for Speed

One Sunday morning I was reading about a book and wanted to get hold of a copy. My options were to drive to the local bookstore (about an hour for the round trip), order it on Amazon (2 days minimum), or get it within 60 seconds on my Kindle. It was a no brainer, I wanted it NOW! And now that I know I can have it now why would I bother waiting for even an hour to get it?

Seven years ago *The Guardian* newspaper warned that we were moving into a society that places a premium on instantaneity; we want to have our wishes granted now. I think we can all agree they were right. How long do you give a TV programme before you decide to flick to another channel? If we can order a ticket, make a payment or get a confirmation online now, more and more of us are opting to do so. And if we want a new book, fewer people than ever are bothering to leaving the house to get it.

Encouraging our poor impulse control is actually not particularly healthy. As our grandparents' generation might have put it, 'waiting is character building' and it's true that those who learn self-control generally do better in most aspects of their lives. You may recall the famous experiment in which researchers offered marshmallows to 4-year olds[20]. One by one each child was brought into a room, given a single marshmallow and told they could eat it. But, said the researcher, I'll be back in fifteen minutes, and if you still have the marshmallow when I return, I'll give you another

---

20   Y. Shoda, W. Mischel and P.K. Peake (1990). 'Predicting Adolescent Cognitive and Self-Regulatory Competencies from Preschool Delay of Gratification: Identifying Diagnostic Conditions', *Developmental Psychology* 26 (6): 978–986.

one. Eat the marshmallow now or save it and get a second one, it's up to you.

The researchers then tracked the lives of those kids for years afterwards. The chief finding: the 30% of kids who didn't eat the marshmallow were more confident, had more friends, got much better grades and better jobs.

But here's the problem. Customers don't want character building; they just want everything now and in most industries you will be severely punished for being slow or late to respond.

Research commissioned by Vodafone suggests that small businesses across Europe are missing out on new business opportunities because they simply can't respond to enquiries fast enough, especially when today's customers expect 24-hour availability.

The research polled a total of 1,000 SMEs in the UK, Germany, Italy and Spain over a 12-week period. It showed that 78% of small businesses perceived rapid response time as their number one source of competitive advantage and 33% blamed a slow response for the loss of contracts.

Half of firms said that in the current business environment, customers' expectations of an instant response to enquiries made across many different channels was the biggest pressure facing their business. They also acknowledged that potential customers were quick to change providers if they didn't get an instant response.

According to the report, SMEs are looking to raise their game by working smarter rather than by taking on new employees. 42% of small businesses are planning to invest in managed communications to make themselves more competitive. This contrasts sharply with the 20% that plan to increase recruitment.

But this issue doesn't just affect SMEs; it affects everyone, at nearly every point of customer interaction.

Even your website is penalised for being slow

Google has included the time it takes your website's landing page to load in its AdWords quality score. Fast loading websites are rewarded, whereas the slow coaches are penalised with higher ad costs. Google says: "Users value ads that bring them to the information they want as efficiently as possible. A high-quality landing page should load quickly as well as feature unique, relevant content. Fast load times benefit advertisers as well, since users are less likely to abandon a site that loads quickly".

Today 71% of consumers expect websites to load as quickly on their smartphones as they do on their home computers. This survey data from Compuware also shows that 74% of mobile phone users won't wait more than 5 seconds for a page to load before abandoning it and moving on[21].

Great Expectations

In a global study of customer reactions to service delivery, this time carried out by Accenture, only 8% of customers agreed they were highly satisfied with the time taken to completely resolve their problems; down 4% on the previous year. Only 7% said they were highly satisfied with the time they had to wait to be served, either on the phone or in person; this is down 3%. And only 6% said they were

---

21   Compuware Survey July 2011 http://cpwr.it/TPchange11

highly satisfied with customer services being available at convenient times[22].

Clearly the increasing gap between customer expectations and service delivery is a widespread problem, yet many executives are deluded about the actual time taken to respond to consumers. In a study by Bain & Company, 80% of senior managers believed their company was doing an excellent job of serving its customers. Only 8% of their customers agreed.

So the conclusion is clear. Your customers can sit at home on a Sunday morning and get a new book in their hands within 60 seconds. The global marketplace is training your customers to expect to get what they want faster and easier. And if you don't keep up with the pace of change and learn methods to deliver faster responses you will pay the price.

Summary

The ease and speed with which some organisations are serving their customers is causing high expectations across the board. The result is that when customers don't get what they want when they want it they're more likely to complain than ever before. Furthermore, they won't just tell a few friends; today's complaints are public and can be permanent. As a result, many companies are finding it more difficult and costly to manage their reputation. And it's not only customers that aren't happy. Over half of the staff employed in the UK today don't like where they work. And when staff members are unhappy it has an impact on customers, which impacts loyalty and costs.

---

22   *The 2010 Accenture Global Consumer Research Survey*, http://bit.ly/TPchange4

Which leaves us with two unanswered questions:

1) What to change?

2) How to change it?

What to Change – 4 Key Strategies

Strategy 1: Be obsessed with customer happiness

In 2004 Laurence Barrett was the Executive Director of
VELUX in the UK. Being Executive Director of the Danish
window manufacturer was, on paper, a dream job. The
company was the number one supplier of roof windows in
the world. Despite attempts to break into the market by
other suppliers, most of whom were providing windows at
a cheaper price, VELUX dominated. The company had the
highest market share and a healthy margin. Most directors
would have put their feet up and enjoyed the enviable
position of being the market leader. But Barrett wasn't
content.

He was aware of a constant undercurrent of customer
dissatisfaction. The situation was brought to a head when
a disgruntled customer sent a recorded delivery letter to
every director of the company. The letter arrived at each
director's home on a Saturday morning and caused uproar
on the Monday morning.

"The letter" as Barrett remembers "was a turning point; it
brought the poor service issues to a head and gifted me the
support to investigate the full extent of the problem and, as
we were to find, there was definitely a problem."

Vanguard Scotland was called in to help. Our first move
was to put together a team of frontline VELUX UK staff to
analyse the nature of customer contact demand and study
the value created for the customer. It was discovered that
the level of failure demand was around 45% and Barrett
recalls that "it was evident that the customer was getting

the run around. Only 52% of our calls were handled in one stop (i.e. by the first person they spoke to). We had so many different lines and so many different service desks, each with their own functional area of responsibility, that the customer service agents had become accustomed to first checking if the customer had got to the correct desk rather than solving their problem."

The company also had an incentive scheme for operators to upsell window blinds. This simply exacerbated the problem. Operators were listening for customers who were ready to buy; any callers with questions not related to an immediate sale were passed off to other areas. To make matters worse, once the question had been answered, if the customer then made a request to purchase, they would get passed back to yet another agent in the service centre.

Barrett took action fast. On the day he got the information about the effects of the call centre design and the incentive scheme he put a new pay structure into place and started to run experiments to see how many calls could be handled in one stop if a combination of skills were used to deal with the customer. Initially two people would take the call together, each with the ability to listen to the customer demand and respond.

Within a few months the call centre was handling nearly all calls in one stop. Within three years Barrett had replaced the fourteen different functional service desks with one desk that could handle any demand. And, in an independent survey, positive customer ratings had increased by 40%. The bottom line improved by over £1m. The following research explains why.

Why good service makes good financial sense

As early as 1994, a group of Harvard professors (Heskett *et al*)[23] found that there was a significant relationship between service and an organisation's key business indicators. For example they found that even a small increase in customer loyalty of 5% could generate an increase in profits of between 25% and 80%. They explain the relationship thus: "The service profit chain establishes relationships between profitability, customer loyalty, employee satisfaction and productivity. The links in the chain are as follows: profit and growth are stimulated by customer loyalty and loyalty is a direct result of customer satisfaction. The simple reason is that more loyal customers purchase more."

As part of their research the Harvard team studied data from Xerox. Management at the copier company were interested in the buying habits of customers who were satisfied versus those that were very satisfied. What they found was that the 'very satisfied' customers at the top of the happiness scale bought six times more product than those that were just 'satisfied'. So when Laurence Barrett was engineering better service it was, according to the researchers, inevitable that the company would make more money.

Other studies have found similar results. Seminal studies using the PIMS (Profit Impact of Market Strategy) data set show significant associations between service quality, marketing variables and profitability. Findings from these studies show that companies offering superior service achieve higher than normal market share growth, that the mechanisms by which service quality influences profits include increased market share and premium prices and

23   J. Heskett , T. Jones, G. Loveman, E. Sasser, A. Schlesinger (April 1994) 'Putting the Service Profit Chain to Work', *Harvard Business Review*

that businesses in the top quintile of relative service quality on average realise 8% higher prices than their competitors.

Other well-known companies have also proved the theory works. American Express found profits rose 8% when it improved service and online shoe retailer Zappos used the philosophy to build the company's value from zero to nearly a billion dollars in just ten years. Zappos' CEO Tony Hirsh asserts that the company's obsession with customer satisfaction was its main market differentiator and the key reason for growth.

Unlike other organisations, Zappos encourages customers to call its call centres and has no targets for sales or call handling time. In fact they celebrate agents that can engage the customer; Hirsh proudly says that their longest single call to one customer lasted over five hours. They also offer free shipping, for both deliveries and returns, and encourage their customers to buy up to six pairs of shoes at once and return the ones they don't like. These are the kind of practices that would make a typical UK call centre manager lose control of their bowels. Yet Zappos was recently sold to Amazon for $998 million, with Jeff Bezos, Amazon's CEO, claiming that nothing would be changed about the company. In an interview, Bezos explained that he bought the company because he gets all weak-kneed when he sees a truly customer-obsessed company[24].

According to MSN money and Zogby International, companies with top service awards also make good on profits. Nordstrom shares are up almost 200% this decade. In 1989, Trader Joe's had $150 million in sales; in 2010 the figure was $2.7 billion. Google shares are up more than 450% since its 2004 initial public offering.

---

24   You can watch the video interview here: http://bit.ly/TPchange12

Conversely, the 2010 Accenture Global Consumer Survey found that 64% of consumers switched their business away from at least one of their service providers due to poor customer service in 2010[25].

In summary, becoming obsessed with making customers happy makes good financial sense. And even a small improvement can have a dramatic effect on customer loyalty, leading to more revenue through repeat purchases. But, let's be honest, you knew that already – didn't you?

---

25   *The 2010 Accenture Global Consumer Research Survey*, http://bit.ly/TPchange4

Strategy 2: Be obsessed with staff happiness

Five years ago, for my 40th birthday, my wife allowed me to go to New York with an old pal. Though I'm not much of a shopper I did want to get a shirt whilst I was in the city. I went to Saks at 5th Avenue and found the shirt department. Within a few moments an assistant, named Alex, came over to greet me. But he didn't just say hi, he reached out his hand, shook mine, and gave me his business card. Only then did he ask if he could be of service. I said I wanted a blue, Boss, easy-iron shirt. He checked the stock and after five minutes came back with two.

I asked if I could try the shirts on but found the sleeves were a bit too long; "No problem", he said, "let me have them altered and I'll have them sent to your hotel". And whilst arranging this he got me a cold drink.

I ended up spending $450 in that shop on shirts, ties, jeans and shoes. I only went in for a shirt. But that wasn't the best bit. He asked if I had a business card. I gave him an old one I had in my wallet. When I got back home he had sent me a thank you card. And every Christmas since then he's sent me a card. When I go back, guess where I'll be going to buy my clothes?

Whilst spending lots more money than I'd planned, I asked him if he enjoyed his job. His reply: "I love my job". Once again, it may seem obvious, but happy staff are good for business.

And it's not just common sense; studies show that motivated staff help a company to make more money, grow and assist in keeping costs down.

A recent study of a franchise system in Europe made up of 933 employees and 50 outlets found that levels of customer happiness were reflected by levels of staff happiness. They also found that customers are twice as likely to buy from an outlet when employees are satisfied as when they are not. The researchers called this the 'double positive effect' – the company gains in the first instance by having happy staff, this leads to happier customers and the happier the customers become the more likely they are to buy something[26].

Going back to our earlier research on the service profit chain, the authors lay out what's happening through the whole process. Heskett *et al* showed that profit and growth are primarily stimulated by customer loyalty; loyalty is a direct result of customer satisfaction; satisfaction is influenced by the value of services provided to customers; value is created by satisfied and loyal employees; which in-turn results in processes, policies and managerial support that help employees to help the customer... get it?

Let me put it in simpler terms: the reason why I bought so much stuff from this New York retailer was because Alex was happy – which made me happy. Because I was happy I spent more and Alex was happy because the design of the work allowed him to give great service. The moral of this story is that the next time I'm out shopping I'm going to look for someone surly to serve me.

Which leads us to the next natural question: what is it that makes employees happy? Thankfully the Hungarian

---

26 H. Evanskitzky, C. Groening, M. Vikas, M. Wunderlich (May 2011) 'How Employer and Employee Satisfaction Affect Customer Satisfaction: An Application to Franchise Services', *Journal of Service Research*

psychologist Mihaly Csikszentmihaly[27] has been studying this question for the past 30 years, so he can point us in the right direction. He says that there are four conditions required to put employees into a state of 'flow' or optimum happiness at work, these are:

1) Employees must be challenged to the maximum of their capabilities

2) Employees must receive immediate and meaningful feedback on their performance

3) Employees must be able to influence other parties in their work processes

4) Employees must be able to see the result of their actions both up and down stream; in other words, they must be able to see how their actions affect the customer

Dan Pink's work on human motivation, *Drive: The Surprising Truth About What Motivates Us*, backs this up further. Dan asserts that the secret to high performance and satisfaction – at work, at school, and at home – is the deep human need to direct our own lives, to learn and create new things, and to improve ourselves and our world. He concludes that the three elements of true motivation are autonomy, mastery and purpose and that the carrot and stick performance incentives traditionally used in business can actually be counterproductive and get you worse results in the long term. For manual labour, assembly lines, etc., the good old reward scheme will work perfectly and get you what you want. But for tasks which require any thought, even simple customer interactions, your typical

---

27   M. Csikszentmihalyi (1990) *Finding Flow – The psychology of optimal experience*, New York: Harper & Row

monetary motivational scheme will lead to poorer overall performance. These findings have been replicated again and again by psychologists, sociologists and economists at some of the world's most prestigious institutions. It's a hard concept for many to accept but I urge you to look into it. Some of the world's most successful companies use this approach to managing staff motivation: Google, for example. And speaking of Google, Dan's findings are brilliantly conveyed in a 10-minute, RSA Animates video on YouTube. I'd recommend Googling it...

In a recent book called *The Dragonfly Effect*, authors Jennifer Akers and Sandy Smith cite similar conditions needed to make people shiny and happy at work[28]. The first thing that they explain is that we're confused about what makes us happy. It's not more money or a new Maserati. The happiest people chase meaning not money. At some point in our lives (normally starting in our thirties), we start to look for a more purposeful existence. And the authors claim that even small changes can have a big impact (the ripple effect). But what should we change to become happy? Interestingly it's very simple – just take small actions that have a significant impact on others. So when a VELUX employee is encouraged to do everything to resolve a customer complaint or meet a customer demand in one stop, they're not just making the customer happy – they're inadvertently becoming happier themselves. And, as we already know, happier staff give better service which breeds loyalty; so it becomes a virtuous circle. Everybody, including the company, wins!

So what do we know so far? That it makes good business sense to delight customers and to delight staff. We also know that service happens at any point of transaction

---

28   J. Akers, and S. Smith (2010) *The Dragonfly Effect*, Stanford, CA: Stanford Education

with the customer and that in that moment people make a judgement about your organisation, reputation and ultimately your brand. But in many environments the initial transaction is merely a commitment to deliver a promise to the customer, which leads us to the next business strategy. When you have a promise to deliver you'd better do it fast.

Strategy 3: Be obsessed with speed of response

It makes good commercial sense to manage throughput and deliver a fast response. Let's return to Zappos, the US internet shoe and clothing giant, for a moment. The online retailer makes a point of trying to take an order late at night and, as a result of exploiting time zones, have the product sitting on the customer's doorstep when they get up in the morning. CEO Tony Hirsh believes that their focus on speed is another reason for their growth and high profitability. He cites the case of one woman who enjoyed the experience so much that she spent over $62,000 on shoes. Whether or not the speed of delivery had anything to do with that particular case cannot, of course, be proven.

Ben Waller and Geoff Williams provide further evidence of the benefits of speed[29], and how it can be used to advantage during times of market change. Companies like Kodak and Dell grew at a time when the world was just realising that it simply couldn't wait for anything longer than the time it takes to for a rain shower to appear in Scotland (faster than the time it takes a butterfly to flap its wings).

For example, in 2001 Dell achieved a 40% growth in business (compared to only 15% growth for its competitors) by delivering faster; and Kodak saw market share rocket from 5% to 40% over the 1980s and 90s by being the first to offer instant photo processing.

The research also supports the evidence that faster makes commercial sense. In their classic book *Competing against Time*, authors George Stalk and Thomas M Hout maintain

---

29   G. Williams, and B. Waller (2010) 'Do customers want instant gratification? Lessons from other industries' *Executive Briefing*

that reducing time in a process by 50% will reduce your costs by 25%[30]. In fact Dell claims a 50% cost advantage compared to its competitors. And in a world that values being first, Toyota won the race to bring the first hybrid car to market, producing the Prius in just 15 months, enabling it to dominate sales in the eagerly waiting market. And if you need any more evidence to support the belief that being slow costs you more and gets you less, dare I mention the Edinburgh tram fiasco. Project slow coach has recently gone over budget by £395 million.

So why is faster better? The first reason, as I've explained, is that consumers are not willing to wait any more. But also, as you streamline and speed up processes, it stands to reason that less waste (rework, duplication, errors, etc.) should be generated, therefore more capacity is created. That capacity can be used to handle more work or can simply be taken as cost savings by reducing resources.

The most famous example of waste reduction occurred at Toyota. The 1990 study of the car industry by Professors Jones and Womack generated the now famous statistic that the number of man hours it takes to make a Lexus is less than the man hours required just to rework a top-of-the-range luxury German car at the end of the line after it has been made. The net effect of the Toyota time-based approach was vastly reduced operating expense. So far we've talked a lot about the US and Europe, but what about the UK? Are there opportunities here to remove waste and improve throughput times? I believe this next example proves the point nicely.

---

30   G. Stalk Jr, T.M. Hout (2003) *Competing Against Time*, New York: Free Press

Findings from the UK public sector

Audit Scotland recently announced that the Scottish criminal justice system was costing the country £56 million in inefficiencies.

Elsewhere, other efforts towards efficiency savings were being made. Alex Salmond, the Scottish First Minister, announced that the current design of eight regional Scottish police forces would be merged into one national force; the objective being more effectiveness and more efficiency. The projected savings come from fewer senior staff and the sharing of backroom activities.

In my opinion the First Minister has missed a trick. Had he started by studying the flow of the criminal justice system he'd have found even more ways to create capacity and free up money, which could be used to put more bobbies on the beat.

In 2007 Colin Peebles, the then Director of Corporate Services at Lothian and Borders Police, had a big idea – improve throughput, and hence reduce costs, in Scotland's summary justice system. We were fortunate to be asked to support a team of front line officers, procurators fiscal, court officers, social workers and admin staff who worked tirelessly to study over 11,000 cases that had been tried in the West Lothian justice system.

Here are the facts about the performance of that system at the time:

- In West Lothian an average of 13 cases were created per day.
- Accused people always left the custody suite not knowing when they would attend court.

- Despite a service standard of 28 days for producing a police report, the actual available capacity meant it could take up to 120 days (the fault of the standard not the officer).
- 50% of accused individuals didn't enter any plea at their first appearance at court. In 36% of those cases the defendant's agent had not been given the details of their crime.
- 65% of those who did not enter a plea went to two pleading courts; 22% went to three.
- At the intermediate court date (the purpose of which is to plead or proceed to trial) 16% of those attending required a further date and another 25% required a further intermediate court and trial. Some of the reasons were: police statements not available, Legal Aid not in place and agents not prepared.
- 15% of those that required a further intermediate court date eventually had another four.
- At the trial, 26% required another trial and had to go back for an intermediate court date. The reasons were: non-appearance of civilian witness (26%), lack of court time (24%).
- 53% of those who did not plead or go to trial required two trials, 28% required three, 11% required four or more and 8% required five or more trials
- As a result of all this, a judgement could take up to 473 days, or 1.3 years.

Most of this was avoidable. In fact it occurred as a direct result of the design and management of the system. I'm not suggesting that we ask accused people what they would like and provide some sort of 5-star service. But, if the system did what it was supposed to, and management stopped tampering with the processes, service would be better/ faster and costs would be less.

We went ahead and asked the local leadership and front-line staff to help us prove this. Both the leadership and the team collaborated to change the work design and achieved the following:

Reduced times from arrest to fiscal marking[31]:

- 150 days to 59 days (21 weeks to 8 weeks) for any general case in the system, regardless of marking
- 197 days to 94 days for a case marked to court, either Sheriff or District
- 100 days to 36 days for any non-court disposal of a case

Reduced times from arrest to case disposal:

- From 472 days to 202 days for any general case in the system (57% faster)
- From 607 days to 233 days for a case marked to either court (62% faster)
- From 320 days to 110 days for any non-court disposal of a case (66% faster)

Additionally:

- 70% of all cases were concluded in under 90 days
- 75% of project reports were error free, in comparison to 20% in the previous system

The important point about this study is that, by working on reducing time taken, without introduction of errors, you are forced to remove wasteful processes from the system and

---

31 Fiscal marking is the term given to the decision reached by the procurator fiscal on whether to prosecute an accused individual.

thereby create more capacity. The spare time can be taken as direct resource savings or be used to do more 'value work'[32]. This verifies in practice Stalk and Hout's statements about the relationship between time and money savings which I referred to earlier.

But the last word on this subject should be left to the man known for creating the best ever example of time-based improvement. Improvements that resulted in the lowest operating expense, fastest time and highest quality in car production ever seen in the car industry.

In a book written just before his death, the creator of the Toyota production system and then CEO of the company, Taiichi Ohno, was asked what he focused on. His answer was simple, "reducing the time from receipt of the order to receipt of the money".

---

32   Value work is the work that is related to the purpose of an organisation from the customer's perspective.

Strategy 4: Be obsessed with constant innovation

Underpinning all of the other three strategies is the need to develop a system that supports the need for constant improvement. Better service, better morale and faster response are all primarily features of work design. Therefore, it stands to reason that as changes in the market, technology and demographics all take hold, the organisation needs to be able to respond to them better. That is why organisations need a method that enables them to lead change. This is the process of constant innovation. And seemingly the lack of it is keeping some of us up at night.

According to the April 2011 edition of *The Economist*, Barack Obama's number one concern is the lack of innovation in the West. He worries, the newspaper says, that the next breakthroughs in energy, transportation and information technology will come from elsewhere[33]. And he'd be right to worry.

Cited in the same article, a Gallup poll highlighted a shift in world opinion on who holds worldwide economic power. China is now assumed to be the dominant force and *The Economist* says it is the country's absolute commitment to innovation that has caused the swing. Since 2008, the share of GDP that China devotes to research and development has doubled. In 2009 the proportion of GDP committed to innovation finally outstripped that in the US.

The outlook for the West seems gloomy then. But maybe we'd get better if we were more aware of the circumstances that drive innovation.

---

33   G, Ip. (28/04/2011) 'Still full of ideas but not making jobs', *The Economist*, http://econ.st/ TPchange13

Examples of the need for innovation

So when might innovation be necessary? The late management guru Peter Drucker[34] cites seven occasions:

Unexpected occurrences: such as the need for renewable energy. This being the catalyst causing the Scottish Government to invest heavily in wind and wave farms.

Incongruities: when a fixed belief turns out to be wrong. For example many managers turn away from targets when they realise their destructive effect on human behaviour.

Process needs: for example a local government grants process that had to be reformed because it was taking over one thousand days to deliver a service for the elderly.

Industry and market changes: the growth of the domestic solar panel industry was fuelled by the government's decision to pay incentives to create energy for the power grid.

Demographic changes: for instance, as a country's population lives longer, there is a need for new processes and policies to support the growing elderly population.

Changes in perception: a call centre manager sees that customers get a bad experience as a result of the organisation's focus on productivity and sees, as a result, the need to change its measurement system.

New knowledge: such as the hybrid car which could not have been built until the technology existed to make it.

Drucker also explains that innovation itself should be a process. He claims that we're less likely to find it from

---

34   P. Drucker (1985) *Innovation and Entrepreneurship, Practice and Principles.* New York. Harper & Row

flashes of genius in our ivory towers than from getting down and dirty in the trenches. Further, he advises that we need systems and practices that actually seek out opportunities to innovate. Finally he reminds us that, unlike the decision to make Edinburgh tram-friendly, the best innovations are those that start small. More brass tacks than tram tracks. Let's look at a case that started from small beginnings and went on to market domination.

Innovation at work

In 1990, Forrester Adam joined a wood turning company as a job estimator. The company at the time was operating out of a glorified shed in a backwater on the east coast of Scotland. But after Forrester led the management buyout of the company in 2001 his enthusiasm and never-ending desire to innovate in every aspect of business was virtually guaranteed to bring it success.

The first opportunity came from demographic and lifestyle changes. In the late 80s and early 90s more companies got interested in how their buildings looked and wanted to create a better working environment. Forrester's company, Haldane, was supplying glazing beads (the wood that keeps a window in a door). The standard market option was square but customers no longer wanted square. They wanted windows to be round, oblong and dolphin-shaped (who knows?). Haldane saw an opportunity to innovate, took a leap, invested in new technology that enabled any shape to be built and delivered as a single bead, then pinpointed interior designers and architects as key market influencers, changing its messaging and marketing to match. The company stole a march on the market of at least five years. Forrester was so protective of the new process that when clients came to visit he covered the machines that made the product so no one could steal it.

Haldane also manufactured handrails for hotels and shopping centres. And these clients also wanted more varied designs. So, driven by the need to be first and different, Forrester then developed systems that allowed solid blocks of wood to literally turn corners. He also constantly changed the little stuff. For example, by listening to the fitter who built the handrails on site, he realised that the packaging needed to be labelled so that each box could be opened in the right order and that the handrail parts needed to be marked so that they would be easier to fit together (a bit like building a Lego model).

Over the years Forrester and his team have changed their scheduling systems, their processes for providing drawings to the shop floor and their CNC machines. At every step of the way, first and foremost was the customer's need and experience. It was worth it.

So far, Forrester's team has won a string of awards including The Queen's Award for Enterprise and a matching string of prestigious contracts including Windsor Castle, Euro Disney, The British Embassy in Moscow, Bluewater shopping centre and The Overgate Centre in Dundee.

Innovation pays and, as Drucker says, the most important aspect of innovation is to have it built into your DNA; if Forrester's could be cloned he could probably make money from that too. And maybe that's his next innovation.

We've covered a lot so far – the need for change, the benefits of change and strategies for change. Or to put it simply, the why and the what of change. But you also need to know the 'how to' bit. That's next.

How to Cause the Change

So far I've argued that organisations, both in the public and private sectors, need four strategies to survive and thrive, let's recap:

Strategy 1: Be obsessed with customer happiness

Strategy 2: Be obsessed with staff happiness

Strategy 3: Be obsessed with speed of response

Strategy 4: Be obsessed with constant innovation

Which begs two questions:

1) What needs to be changed?

2) How should the change be caused?

Most organisations see these issues as being mutually exclusive, i.e. each one should have its own initiative. For the rest of the book I'm going to argue that in fact they're connected, and the causal factor in whether you succeed in each area is how you think about, manage and design your organisation. So the key change needs to be at the level of management thinking, not at the level of individual projects or initiatives.

It's at this stage that I may upset you. Simply because my recommendations are a departure from the well trodden path, a bit like being told that to slim down you really need to eat more chocolate. What's more, I'm going to suggest that in the UK the common methods used to achieve organisational change are likely to make the situation worse, not better.

The need for knowledge

The problem with the Coke taste test, it was later suggested, was that the testers didn't know that they were testing for a new Coke. Had Gay Mullins known that he was voting for a change when he took the taste test – that he was voting to scrap the old-style Coke that he loved – he most likely would have rejected the new recipe. The mistake that Coca Cola executives made was that they based their decision to change solely on the taste results, without real knowledge of their customers' attitudes towards old Coke. They were working with only part of the picture.

Making change without knowledge is, from an organisational perspective, one of the biggest problems we face in the UK today. Consider these examples:

Assuming you know the causes

The management of a finance system assumed that the poor throughput time they were seeing was due to communication and structural issues (although poor communication was merely a consequence of work design, not a cause). But they ploughed on with a programme of workshops designed to promote vision, mission and values. One of the values was the concept of the internal customer. This is a flawed concept. There is only one customer that the organisation should be serving, that's the one that pays for the service. The concept was designed to promote internal harmony and better communication; it made it worse. In-fighting ensued as staff jockeyed for position in the queue arguing over who should be given priority. The real loser was the end customer.

Not knowing how to look for the causes

Audit Scotland recently announced it had completed its review of the effect of 3 years of legislative change designed to save money and improve performance in local authority planning departments. It found that both had actually got worse. But nowhere in their report did they say what the causes were. The government's assumptions were that costs could be saved by accepting applications via the internet and by providing pre-application advice. In a study of four local authority planning departments we found that neither change had made any difference to the service. In fact, there was evidence to suggest that the pre-application process had caused agents to seek free advice that they might previously have paid for; the result was higher operating expense and lower income. Furthermore, end-to-end time for all aspects of the service (pre-application, determinations and discharge of conditions) continued to rise even after the implementation of the internet application system. The causes were missed. In this sort of environment, a casework system, multi-tasking, setting of targets and constantly shifting priorities all have to be challenged in order to make a change to the system.

Acting to make things worse

In Figure 1 you'll see a graph for a housing system. Each vertical point on the graph measures the time from a request for a repair to completion of that repair. You don't need a degree in statistics to see the trend in performance; it's clearly getting worse. An assumption had been made that the imposition of a service standard (10 days) would improve the time from receipt of the order to completion of the repair. The first jobs (at the start of the graph) show the system prior to the change. But as management imposed

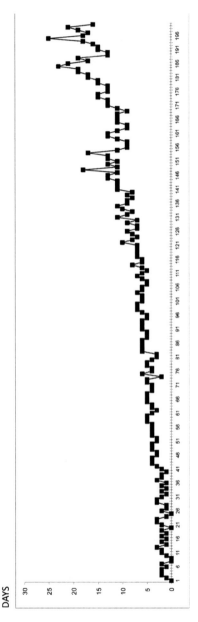

Figure 1: Time from request to completion of a repair in a housing system.

the new service standard the time to close a job increased. This happened because staff were now working to the standard rather than doing what was right for the customer i.e. 'we now have 10 days to do the work'. This is reflected on the graph by the rising data points.

Because management were looking at the data in a linear format they could not see that the performance of the service was declining. So when they created this chart they got a shock. It's something that you always learn when you measure true end-to-end times in services that work to standards. The imposition of an arbitrary measure actually 'tampers' with the system, making variation increase and service deteriorate.

Managers don't see the real performance because they rarely look at their data over time and in the form of a trend. Further, because they look at performance against a standard, the variation in a process is hidden.

Too little knowledge is evidently a dangerous thing; a lot of it however is an incredibly powerful tool.

How to get knowledge

Assuming then that you accept that change starts with knowledge, you have to know how to get knowledge.

Perspective

The first part of knowledge is perspective, meaning the way that you look at an organisation. As I said earlier, better service is cheaper and is good for growth and profits; so it's critical that you see your organisation or service in the same way that a customer sees it.

Here's an example. A few years ago my bank delivered a great service. I used to be able to speak to one person who could do everything for me. In that single transaction I could access my business account, transfer money to my personal account and then pay bills.

Then, I assume, some boffin in management got concerned with costs and, thinking that trying to manage costs was the way to go, made the following changes:

1) The bank functionalised its call centres, splitting them into one for corporate and one for personal banking. I assume the thinking was that it could get cheaper people. But service got worse and customer loyalty reduced. The many customers like me who used the bank for both types of accounts now had to work twice as hard and long to get the services they needed.

2) It invested in voice recognition and a touch tone service. Now in order to do what I want to do I have to first work my way around the machine.

3) It reduced the hours the corporate call centre is open, despite a TV advertising campaign that says '24-hour call centres'. If you're a business customer of my bank, apparently Gordon Gekko was wrong; money does sleep after all – between 8pm and 8am.

Now from the perspective of the customer, in this case me, these new policies have reduced the previously excellent service levels to the point where I'm thinking of jumping ship, and I certainly wouldn't recommend the bank to other prospective customers. If, as I suspect, I'm not alone, then these new cost-saving policies are in danger of throwing the baby out with the bathwater.

Profits in this bank are down, unlike First Direct which has seen a surge in new customers and profits. It's not a coincidence that it also ranked number one for customer satisfaction in the latest JD Power & Associates UK Retail Banking Satisfaction Study, was the top financial company in the Nunwood Customer Experience Top 100 of 2010, won 13 MoneyWise customer service awards and was named the best current account provider at the 2011 Consumer Moneyfact Awards. According to its own surveys of incoming customers more than 1 in 4 are joining because of a personal recommendation.

Purpose

Having decided that you're going to view the world the way a customer does, you then have to ask a very simple question from the customer's perspective: 'what's the purpose of this system?'

Purpose is a critically important question because it sets out what you are trying to do and how you are trying to do it. It then guides you to measure how well you are achieving that purpose.

My favourite example of this is the lost and found department. If the purpose of that system is to reunite owners with their goods, you'd want to measure how often and how quickly someone gets their lost item back.

But when working with the department in question we found they didn't have this data (my thanks to Adrian Sprott for allowing me to use this example). As Adrian (the manager) said, "we had information coming out of our ears, but had nothing related to the number of items that actually got back to the owner – I bet most businesses are the same".

The first graph shows the number of umbrellas handed in to the Edinburgh lost property office over a 12 month period (Figure 2).

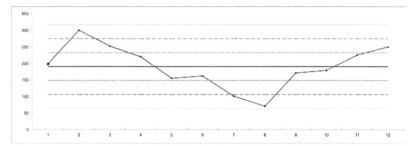

Figure 2: Umbrellas deposited with Lost & Found Dept.

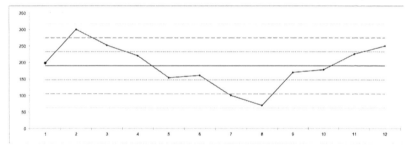

Figure 3: Unclaimed umbrellas thrown away

Figure 3 shows the number that remained unclaimed by their owners. As you can see, there's no difference! In fact, out of the 3,000 umbrellas lost in Edinburgh in this year only one was ever claimed. But each of the other 2,999 went through a 142-step process before later being disposed of in a skip. Another 38,000 items fitted the same profile. Asking 'what's the purpose?' from the customer's perspective allowed Adrian to get a crystal clear picture of what needed to change in his department.

Study the nature of demand

One of the biggest inhibitors to poor service and contributors to high costs is failure demand. If you're joining this book half way through, failure demand is a demand placed on the system as a result of a failure to do something – or a failure to do something right – for the customer. Studying failure demand helps us see which other parts of the system need to be studied and redesigned.

It typically starts with variants of the words:

'You haven't done it yet'

'You haven't done it right'

Or

'Why have you done this to me?'

So you have to study the nature of customer contact demand to see how much is related to the purpose of your system. Typically, as I said earlier, in most organisations we see high levels of failure demand. And most failure is caused by the ways that people design and run organisations.

Managers concerned with costs typically use targets to make people more productive – think call centres, target numbers of calls per hour, etc. But if you're a call centre worker feeling pressured to be more interested in meeting your call-time target than in serving the customer, then service levels will drop and, as a result, failure demand calls will increase (logical right?). And when demand increases, so does cost.

But there's another reason for studying demand. Even if you have no failure demand, you'll want to make sure that you are giving the most appropriate response to the demand you are getting: i.e. you should do no more or less than the customer needs to get great service. As an example, in a council service that collects large bulky items for disposal, we found that 40% of the time the van would have to return to the customer's collection point twice due to the design of the van. The result was a) unhappy customers left wondering why only some of their waste had been collected and b) increased costs due to repeat visits.

Studying demand allows you design the most appropriate response to the incoming request.

Gathering measures related to purpose

Another way of asking 'how well are we achieving our purpose?' is to collect measurements that are related to the purpose of the system from the point of view of the customer. For example, the purpose of local authority planning from its own perspective is to make sure developments meet regulations but, seen from the customer's perspective, this is just red tape formality to be got out of the way as fast as possible so they can get on with their kitchen extension, housing development or whatever. For the customer, the purpose of the department is to confirm if it's OK to proceed as quickly as possible. In which case the planning department needs to know:

How many people ask for, and get, a decision?

How long does it take?

Planning departments in the UK have a target of 57 days or less for making a decision on a planning application. The actual range in the delivery of the decision in the case of four councils we studied was anything up to 166 days. No one knew because, again, they were not looking at their data over time and in the form of a trend graph. In this case the team soon reduced this time to 43 days and, in the process, reduced the associated costs of poor service by £75,000 per annum.

Finding out why it's not working

Knowing what is going wrong is only one part of the equation. You also have to know why it is going wrong. To find out the causes of poor performance you have to study flow (from the point of customer demand to customer fulfilment).

Poor flow of work manifests in many different ways, the main ones being:

- Failure demand
- Rework
- Errors
- Duplication
- Poor quality of information
- Defects
- Poor quality of output
- Slow delivery of service or product

It's not unusual to find up to 50% of the work being done in a process to be wasteful activity, i.e. rework, errors, duplication, hand-offs and information being passed on that is not correct. But seeing the waste in a process is one thing, more important is to know the cause of that waste.

Finding the root cause of the problem

The root causes of waste are not always simple to spot. The problems are caused by the way managers think about the design and management of the work. At business school we're still often taught that organisations should be run as top-down hierarchies, that work should be designed functionally, that targets and service standards should be used to improve productivity and that the job of the manager should be to manage and motivate the workers. John Seddon calls this "the industrialisation of service". And it doesn't work.

One approach that *does* work is known as the Vanguard Method and it's the method we use with service sector clients. Developed by John Seddon, it draws on the approach originally used at Toyota to speed up manufacturing processes, improve quality and, as a result, reduce costs. Service and manufacturing are different but the Vanguard Method starts the process of change in exactly the same way Toyota did: with studying the system. The Vanguard Method then combines two bodies of knowledge: systems thinking principles (for studying and designing service organisations) and intervention theory (for deciding how the change should be made).

This method has proved consistently effective in service organisations, delivering results comparable to Toyota's original economic benchmark. It's based on creating clarity of purpose from the customer's perspective and on designing work against the nature of demand and then making it flow through the system. The aim is to create value for the customer at each point of transaction and to have measures in place that relate to the organisation's purpose. Targets and incentives are eliminated, as are traditional 1:1s and other people-management practices. Instead, the role of management is to take action on the system to encourage constant improvement and optimisation of the service. It is the principles of the Vanguard Method that we are applying and illustrating here.

To recap on the plan of attack:

- First, choose a core business
- Define the purpose of the system from the customer's perspective
- Define measures related to that purpose
- Study customer demand to get data on those measures
- Study the process to identify where there is waste, delay and rework in the workflow
- Identify the policies that are causing that waste
- Get to the root cause of the problems by studying the thinking behind those policies
- Develop a new work design that focuses on getting the work done perfectly from the customer's perspective (and, thereby, reduces waste, delay and rework)
- Run experiments based on the new thinking and work design to test the hypothesis for change
- Study the measures again to see if the changes are working
- Roll the rest of the organisation into the new system

This task list is not a one-off event, it's a constant cycle. While it could be used as a one-time band-aid, that would be short sighted. Trends like the four identified at the start of the book occur all the time, and business history is littered with failed organisations or leaders who didn't notice and act on these sorts of changes.

The only way for a service organisation to become and remain efficient and effective is to know what its customers want now and how well it is delivering it now. And that changes over time.

So this should be a continuing process – a permanent management function. This will allow you to identify changes in real time, so you are always on top of both your costs and your service delivery.

Think about it. How many bureaucratic processes have you encountered in your life that seem to be there for no reason, were put in place because of circumstances that no longer apply or are simply done 'because they've always been done that way'?

These anachronistic processes exist because most of the ways we have been taught to manage (using targets, measuring what's important to the business not the customer, etc.) are flawed and leave organisations vulnerable to high costs and competition.

The model for analysis that we recommend is shown in Figure 4.

Check – Plan – Do

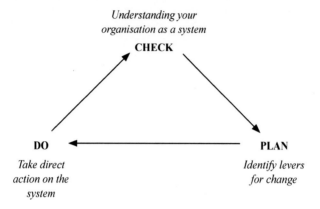

Figure 4: The Vanguard model for analysis

In summary, effective change starts with knowledge. It's why the Vanguard Method is so powerful: only by first diagnosing what's wrong with the current system can you make lasting changes that will improve service and cut costs. However you do need to know the right way to apply the model, as not all services are the same. And that's what I'll look at next.

Categorising Services for Faster Diagnosis

There is a shortcut system you can use to make sure that you apply the model in the right way and that's the approach I'll outline here to keep things simple. In practice, you may need to explore these definitions further. The approach works because some services, even though on the face of it they look different, are actually hybrids of the same type of system.

In service organisations we can group services into three main categories and this makes the analysis and the identification of the solution much faster.

Each category of service has its own points of leverage – two or three factors that determine how work will flow through the system and, as a result, enhance or limit your capacity.

As I've said, to understand the points of leverage you first have to know how to categorise the different types of system. Here are the three main types of service system:

Single-touch Systems:

In this type of service the point of leverage is the possibility of providing the service that the customer is looking for in one stop, without the need for multiple visits, calls, etc. That's what customers want. Housing benefits, revenues, energy bill payments, banking transactions, sports centre bookings and many call centre environments are examples of single-touch systems. The leverage is to shift management's focus from managing people (the 5%) to managing the system (the 95%).

Put-in-to-process Systems:

In this type of system the service cannot be delivered in a single touch; the first point of contact needs to send the work into a process. Think, for example, of building services repairs, mortgage processing, waste collection, pension processing and utility services such as house moves. The leverage is to shift management's focus from managing the work as activity done to a standard time, which creates waste, to creating a system that can absorb variety and focuses on flow of work through the system.

Project Systems:

Like put-in-to-process systems, the customer transaction cannot be completed in one stop and the work is complex; often every piece of work is a 'one-off'. Think, for example, of public sector planning, IT development, building standards, roads resurfacing, gully cleaning, marketing projects and some environmental services like food safety.

The leverage here is to shift management's focus from managing activity to managing capacity and flow and, as I said previously, to remove the causes of poor flow – multi-tasking, targets and constantly shifting priorities.

In the following pages we'll take a look at how this works in practice.

Applying the Model

Case Study 1: A Project System

Release capacity and bring work back in-house to improve speed, service and costs

According to the popular stereotype, the Germans are super-slick and super-efficient. Not always! They are, in fact, just like us; their organisations are prone to the same issues.

The problems are not down to being British or German. Having worked all over Europe and the USA, I can tell you that the problems we face are a Western phenomenon; it's down to how we think about the design and management of work.

This is an issue which was born out of the industrial revolution. We were taught to think that economies of scale, targets and service standards, work functionalisation and top-down approaches to management would give us services that worked better. This may have been true in the age of the Model T Ford ("any colour as long as it's black") but in an age when customers decide what they want and when they want it, the thinking is outdated. Just ask the Germans.

Our first example is taken from work that Daniel Rodgers (a Vanguard Scotland consultant) led. The client, a German car manufacturer, had challenges getting new engines tested on time. Costs were rising, the end-customer was being let down and the company's competitive advantage and brand were being eroded because it was missing product launch dates. This is not, as you may think, manufacturing but a service environment. In this type of service the engine has already been designed and manufactured, it just has to be tested.

If you were to apply our earlier logic by first asking "what type of service is this?" you'd see that each engine is unique, it has to go through a number of different departments, the customer has defined an end date and it has to be managed through the flow – hence it's specifically a project system. This is important because you can now define which elements of the model you want to use to conduct the analysis.

In all environments you always want to start with purpose from the customer's perspective. Here the purpose was, "test the right engine, with the right parts, on time and efficiently". Having defined the purpose the next question to ask is, "how well does the system meet its purpose?"

To answer this question we use capability charts

A capability chart shows how the system is performing over time and the variation in its performance. It can, in this way, predict the limits around which a system will perform. For example, in the capability chart shown overleaf you can see that if you wanted to know how long it takes to test an engine you can only be confident that it will take 128 days or less. As a result the customer's due date was only met 27% of the time.

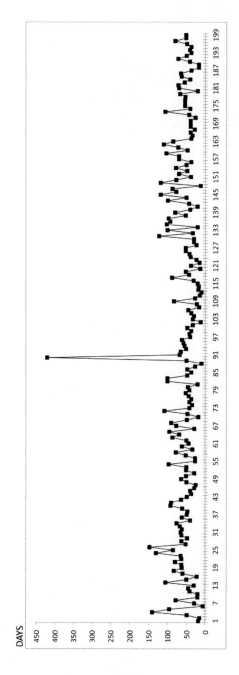

Figure 5: Capability chart – Engine testing end-to-end

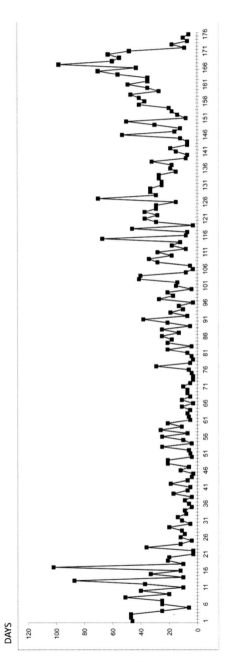

Figure 6: Capability chart – Due date performance

Also, as part of the purpose is to test the right engine with the right part, we wanted know how often the correct combination was tested. This seems like a stupid question (why would you test the wrong engine or the wrong part?). Believe it or not, on 90% of occasions an engine was tested with the wrong part.

It's important to remember that these were not bad managers or people trying to do a bad job, the flaw was simply in their thinking, not in their attitude or intent.

The next stage was to study the process and there were no big issues here, but we didn't expect to find any – it was a project environment. We knew that the problem would be caused by the policies. In project environments there is often a belief that the earlier you start, the earlier you finish, along with a focus on productivity (keep the workers busy). As a result, the system gets flooded with work. The resulting behaviour is multi-tasking; everybody works on lots of little bits of work rather than completing a full task before moving on to the next one. The result is that everything takes longer. To make a change, work would have to be released more slowly into the system – counterintuitive but effective.

The second issue in this system was also related to productivity. Because the system was flooded with work there were not enough benches to test an engine. As a result, a mandate was issued that test benches should be kept busy at all times; and to keep up with demand more were sourced from outside testing facilities. Hiring test benches is expensive work; it costs around €1.5 million per bench per year.

The other reason that benches were so busy was that the mandate drove the workforce to keep engines on a bench unnecessarily or test the wrong engines or parts (remember the earlier stats). This was preferable to letting a bench go idle and receiving a reprimand.

Now we knew what needed to change:

- The number of engines in the flow at any one time
- The mandate that drove people to test the wrong engine and keep a test bench busy

We knew these two simple changes would result in freeing up capacity and, as a result, allow the company to bring all testing back in-house. The saving was calculated to be around €75 million per annum.

Let's recap on our first case study

- We started by asking what kind of system we were going to study
- The clues showed us that it was a project environment
- We then focused on purpose, measures and the work distribution policy
- Only then did we make the change

In the second case study we'll combine how to leverage a process environment with cost savings achieved by reducing non-value added work.

Case Study 2: A 'Put-in-to-process' System

Service improvement, faster delivery, innovation and improvements in staff morale through the reduction of non-value added work

It's very rare that a company designs a process from the customer's perspective.

Ironically, most managers think that better service means more cost – in fact it results in less cost.

Think about it, if you're only doing what matters to the customer and not doing any of the internal stuff designed to satisfy your organisation's needs and wants, then you'll have more capacity and therefore the option of lowering your costs, right?

This next example illustrates this point beautifully.

Whatever age you are right now, imagine yourself as elderly, sick and infirm. Not a pleasant thought is it? If, when you get to that point in your life, you have money, then things may be just fine. But imagine that you're in the position of relying on your local council to make changes and adaptations to your council house just so that you can do basic tasks like getting up and down the stairs and taking a shower in the morning. Then imagine that, when you ask your council for help, you find it's going to take multiple visits and up to 1,185 days to get what you need. You suddenly realise that life will be anything but just fine. Thankfully some councils have grasped the thistle of bad service and are determined to make life better for their communities. In this particular case the local council knew that the service was bad, but they didn't know how bad.

Here you have a hybrid of a process and a project environment, and the leverage was definitely in the process. Again, returning to the model, we started with the purpose. The council's front-line team agreed that the purpose should be: 'To provide an adaptation, fast and efficiently, for qualifying residents'.

So, having established the purpose, this time we started by looking at the nature of demand. We wanted to know if each adaptation was really different and if each needed its own process. What we found was no surprise: most of the adaptations were for level-floor showers, stair lifts and special toilets.

The next step in the model was to see how well the system achieved its purpose; specifically we wanted to know how long it predictably took to complete an adaptation. Much to the dismay of the services' management, we found that it took over 3 years. Fortunately, the people we were working with were determined to change this state of affairs.

The next stage (following the model) was to study the process. (There's a schematic of it in Figure 7.) In brief, a customer calls the council and asks for an adaptation. The first thing that happens is that they get a visit from an occupational therapist, who decides what the customer needs. They are then asked to contact the council again to see if they qualify for financial aid. The forms are all completed and an assessment is done. Unfortunately around 50% of the forms arrive incorrectly completed which causes a delay in processing. Around 40% of people are told at this stage that they will not get financial aid for their adaptation. But the big problem is that months may have passed before they get this news. And the longer it takes to resolve, the more it can cost to help the customer.

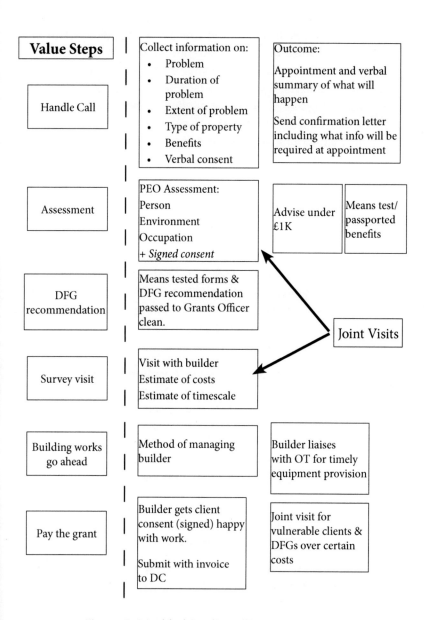

Figure 7: Disabled Facilities Grants Process

Take this example from another council. The daughter of an elderly lady called to say that her mother was a bit lonely and could a lunch club be arranged? It took so long to sort out this simple request that the lady became depressed and then ill; the result was that she needed a visiting carer and meals provided. Eventually, she also got the lunch club. Thus a poor, high costing service was delivered because of a poor response time.

Back to our original council and back to the process map. Those that qualify then get a visit from a council surveyor, who does the necessary drawings. Then a tender is drawn up to appoint a builder. This is done for every case and three quotes must be provided. The most suitable builder is chosen and then the builder visits. Inevitably they then do their own drawings and more time is wasted. In some cases, the customer has waited 9-12 months to get to this stage. Eventually work starts and is signed off by a council employee. The customer can now have a shower.

The front-line team studying this process immediately saw the way to achieve better service and lower costs. "Why not", they said, "have one person who can do the initial analysis and do the means test then put together a team of approved builders?". Though they are working through some legal issues with the procurement process, the new process takes around 20-30 days and costs less money for two reasons:

Earlier intervention means less cost:

On average an elderly person in the UK will enter residential care at around 83 years old. The cost is, on average, £504 per week. The cost of an average stair lift is £1,100, so faster intervention (delaying the need for residential care) will pay for itself very quickly. And the quality of life is generally better for the elderly person.

More capacity means less cost spent on outsourcing:

Some councils use agents to do the drawings for the adaptations. The agents typically charge 15% of the cost of the adaptation. The average cost of a level access shower is currently £4,500, which means the agent gets paid £675 per job. A typical medium-sized council in the UK will do around 260 adaptations per year. If 50% of those are level access showers then bringing the work back in-house can mean a saving of £87,750 every year.

In summary, the point of leverage for this work was the process. Making sure that all the value work was done at the right point in the process was complemented by making sure that those who were in contact with the client had the right skills to do the needs assessment and means testing.

Case Study 3: A Single-touch System

Saving money and improving service in local authority benefits

Assessing whether someone is eligible for housing benefits should be a simple enough process. Actually when you think about it, it shouldn't be a process at all; the transactions should take place in one stop with customer involvement. That's not how it works in practice but thinking of the service as one that can be handled in one stop is the key to making sure that it doesn't cost more than it should.

Again, when you start with the intention of understanding the problem you have to get clear about the purpose of the service, in this case, "to assess my eligibility for benefits and to pay me".

In the council we studied there were over 5,000 new claims per year and over 22,000 changes. The live caseload was over 11,000 and increasing due to the economic downturn. However there were over 125,000 customer contacts per year – and we learned that 77% of these were failure demand.

In other words capacity was being wasted dealing with 96,000 calls every year that would not have been necessary had the system been designed to deliver what mattered to customers.

Once again there were clues all over the system.

It took up to 47 days to assess a new benefits claim and up to 31 days to assess a change of circumstances. 36% of claims contained errors which would affect the claim. And what happened next made the process even more unwieldy.

When a customer made a claim or reported a change, information was collected and passed to the back office.

When assessors got round to processing claims, only 26% had all the information they required to complete the assessment.

The others resulted in a series of letters being sent to the customer for further information.

In fact, in a sample of 50 new claims, customers visited the counter 89 times and made 74 phone calls. However only 3 calls were made to customers and 70 letters and 132 notifications were sent.

Fortunately an enlightened management team immediately saw the holes in the system and a team of front-line staff was charged with redesigning the system. The earlier analysis led them to putting the right skills and knowledge at the front of the system. This made it easy for customers to know what information was required and claims and changes could be processed quickly and efficiently.

The time to assess a new claim has fallen from up to 47 days to up to 16 days, and for a change of circumstances it has fallen from 31 to 7 days.

Customers are happier and failure demand has reduced by half. All in all the capacity release has led to savings of over £120,000.

Summary

To achieve better service at lower costs in these systems you have to follow three simple rules:

- Study the system before making a change. Did you notice that in every case the solution came to light as a result of data from the current performance of the system? We, the management and staff, didn't sit in a room and hypothesise about what we could, should or would do; we were led directly to the solution by the analysis.

- Having studied the system, make sure you make a change. It sounds ridiculous but sometimes, as in the case of the motor manufacturer, the change seems so big that management do nothing and live with the current system. This is again where data helps; it removes emotion from the equation and leaves you with a simple fact: if the method you're currently using gives you X performance, then to get Y performance you have to change the method. As Albert Einstein so famously said, "The definition of insanity is doing the same thing over and over again and hoping for a different result."

- The analysis will be made simpler and quicker by first deciding which type of system you have. In this book I have described three major types of service systems: Single-touch systems, Put-in-to-process systems and Project systems. Knowing which you have and where you can achieve the most change will get you more change: better service, lower costs, more profit and all at less effort.

The biggest challenge for change

The greatest challenge for change is not learning how to analyse a system; it is in how we as leaders think about the design and management of our organisations.

Because we're taught to think about running our organisations based on an outdated industrial model, our service will always tend to be poor and our costs high.

Real change means changing how we think as leaders. Rather than viewing the world top-down from our boardrooms, we must learn to see how things look from the customer's perspective. Rather than designing work functionally, we have to make sure that all customer transactions are value-creating and that the work is made to flow through the system. We must move away from targets, service standards and incentives and move toward measures related to purpose and based on the true capability of the services involved. It is only then that we will be able to achieve what is currently believed to be impossible: lower costs, better service, faster delivery, more innovation, more profits and better conditions for staff.

Resources

To learn more about applying systems thinking management methods, visit the Vanguard Scotland website at www.systemsthinkingmethod.com

About the Author

 Stuart Corrigan is the author of a popular management advice blog on systems thinking and business transformation. He is also the Managing Director of change management consultancy firm Vanguard Scotland Ltd.

Vanguard was founded by Professor John Seddon in 1990 and is a global leader in the provision of change programmes for service organisations. As Vanguard Scotland's most experienced consultant, Stuart has personally led more than 50 successful change programmes across the globe in the last decade for clients ranging from government bodies to household name brands.

Past clients have included Lothian and Borders Police, Powergen, Aon, The Scottish Executive, Royal London Insurance, City of Lincoln Council and Scottish Life.

Stuart's blog and more information about him and Vanguard Scotland – including more case studies, articles, 'how to' videos and eBooks – can be found online at: www.systemsthinkingmethod.com

About Triarchy Press

Triarchy Press is a small, independent publisher of good books about organisations and society - and practical applications of that thinking..

Our authors bridge the gap between academic research and practical experience and write about praxis: ideas in action.

Our books cover innovative approaches to designing and steering organizations, the public sector, teams, society, and the creative life of individuals.

The Vanguard Method

Systems Thinking in the Public Sector – John Seddon

Delivering Public Services that Work Volume 1 – Peter Middleton

Delivering Public Services that Work Volume 2 – Charlotte Pell

Other systems thinking titles:

Systems Thinking for Curious Managers –
Russell Ackoff, with Herbert Addison and Andrew Carey

The Search for Leadership: an organisational perspective –
William Tate

Growing Wings on the Way – Rosalind Armson

Managers as Designers in The Public Services: Beyond Technomagic – David Wastell

www.triarchypress.com

Lightning Source UK Ltd.
Milton Keynes UK
UKOW031045240512

193185UK00001B/6/P